CAMELS

CAMELS

JENNY MARKERT

THE CHILD'S WORLD

DESIGN
Bill Foster of Albarella & Associates, Inc.

PHOTO CREDITS
Leonard Rue III: front cover, 15
COMSTOCK/Janet Wishnetsky: back cover
COMSTOCK/Georg Gerster: 23, 27, 28, 30
COMSTOCK: 19
Dave Wilhelm: 2, 6
Len Rue Jr.: 9, 13, 25
Frank Todd/Ecosystems International: 10
Robert and Linda Mitchell: 17
The Zoological Society of San Diego: 20

Distributed to schools and libraries
in the United States by
ENCYCLOPAEDIA BRITANNICA EDUCATIONAL CORP
310 South Michigan Ave.
Chicago, Illinois 60604

Library of Congress Cataloging-in-Publication Data
Markert, Jenny.
Camels/Jenny Markert.
p. cm. — (Child's World Wildlife Library)
Summary: Describes the characteristics and behavior
of the camel.
ISBN 0-89565-719-8
1. Camels — Juvenile literature.   [1. Camels.]   I. Title.
II. Series.   91-13378
QL737.U54M37 1991   CIP
599.73'6—dc20   AC

For Cindy

The desert is one of the world's most hostile places to live. During the day, the temperature may soar to over 120 degrees, and the ground can fry your feet. Howling winds whip sand and dust in dangerous, biting storms. Except for a few withered bushes and cacti, there is very little to eat in the desert. Finding water is even more difficult than finding food. Few animals can survive such harsh conditions. For the camel, however, the desert is home sweet home.

To many people, camels look strange or funny. Probably the strangest thing about the camel is its hump. People used to think that a camel's hump was filled with water. Now we know that the hump contains fat.

Fat is concentrated in a camel's hump for a very good reason. Unlike camels, people have a layer of fat over their entire bodies. The fat keeps our bodies warm when it's cold outside. Camels, however, must worry more about staying cool than staying warm. If fat were spread over their bodies, camels would quickly overheat in the desert.

A camel's hump serves another purpose, too. The fat in the hump provides the camel with extra fuel. When food is hard to find, a camel uses the fat in its hump for energy. If food is scarce for a long time, a camel's hump can actually disappear! When food is plentiful, the hump becomes big and firm.

Camels have either one or two humps. Those with two humps are called *bactrian* camels. They live in the Gobi Desert, which is in northern China. The Gobi Desert is cold in the wintertime. To survive the cold temperatures, bactrian camels have short legs and shaggy fur. Their short legs save heat when it's cold outside. Their thick fur helps keep them warm, too.

Camels with one hump are called *dromedary* camels. They live in the deserts of Arabia, India, and North Africa. Temperatures in these regions are hot all year long. Dromedary camels have short fur that keeps their skin cool. They also have long, thin legs that allow heat to escape from their bodies. The long legs help keep the dromedary's body away from the hot ground, too.

Both bactrian and dromedary camels have built-in protection from desert sandstorms. They have long eyelashes that keep sand and dust out of their eyes. Camels also have extra eyelids that work like windshield wipers. They slide over the camel's eyes and push sand and dust out of the way.

Camels have other features that protect them from sandstorms. They have small ears that are covered with hair. The hair keeps blowing sand out of their ears. To keep sand out of their mouths, camels can clamp their lips tightly shut. Camels even have special muscles that can close their nostrils!

Surviving sandstorms is not the only problem in the desert. Finding food is also a chore. Although they prefer moist leaves and grass, camels eat whatever they can find. They have thick, rubbery lips, so they can eat dry bushes and prickly thorns. A hungry camel also will eat bones, leather, and man-made tents!

After a meal of wilted leaves and thistles, most animals would love a drink of water. However, water is not an easy thing to find in the desert. Camels get some water from the plants they eat. When camels come across a water hole, they usually drink a lot. In an entire day, a camel can drink 50 gallons of water. That's enough water to fill a large bathtub!

After drinking so much water, camels can wait a long time until they get thirsty again. In the winter, they can go six months without a single sip of water!

Baby camels do not have to worry about where to find their next drink. They get all the milk they can drink from their mothers. The milk supplies them with the nutrients they need to grow. Female camels have only one baby at a time. That way, the baby camel has all the milk it needs to be healthy.

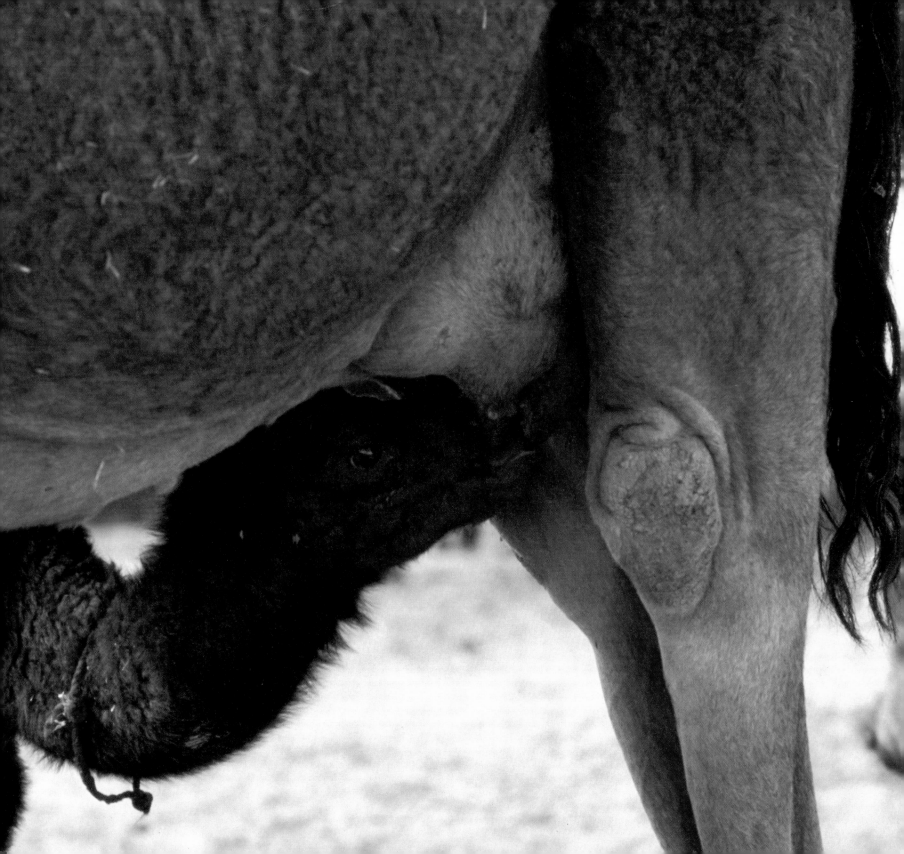

Mother camels have lots of help raising their young. Wild camels live in herds that contain between 10 and 20 animals. All of the members of the herd help protect the young camels. By the time they are two years old, the young camels can survive on their own. However, they usually stay with the same herd that they grew up with.

Because the camel is so well adapted to life in the desert, people have used them for thousands of years. Desert nomads use camels for many different purposes. People weave camel's hair into clothes and tents. They use the camel's skin to make tough leather shields and saddles. People also drink camel's milk. On special occasions, desert nomads even eat camel meat.

Although camels serve many purposes, they are used most widely as a means of travel. In some places, camels are still the only way to carry heavy loads through the desert. On short hauls, a camel can carry up to 1,000 pounds. That's more than an elephant can carry! However, camels can be stubborn helpers. They know exactly how much they can lift. If a load is too heavy, a camel will grunt, groan, and make terrible faces. If a camel is angered or tired, it will spit, bite, and trample on its handler's feet.

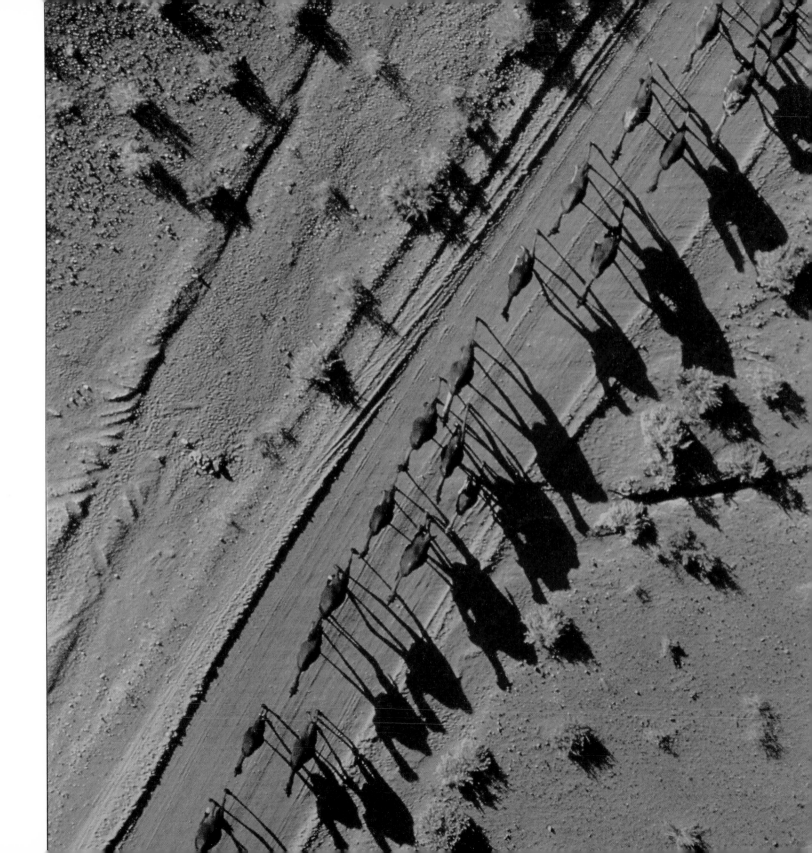

Despite their short tempers, camels are important companions of people who live in the desert. Without the camel, people could not prosper in the scorching heat and endless sand. Even more than humans, camels have conquered one of the harshest habitats on earth. They can survive the extreme heat, drought, and lack of food. They are perfectly designed for life in the desert.